TIME WILL TELL

An Easter Play

BY

KATHLEEN MORRIS

Rouge Publishing

Rouge Publishing

ISBN 978-1-927828-23-6

OTHER BOOKS BY KATHLEEN MORRIS

Deep Bay Series
Deep Bay Vengeance
Deep Bay Relic
Deep Bay Legacy (Coming 2014)
Blood War Series
The Prion Attachment
Blood Purge (Coming 2014)
Short Inspirations Series
Size Seven Shorts
Short End Of The Stick
Shortcut To Alaska
Short Stories
Along The Way - 12 Short Stories You Can
Read Along The Way
Plays
Time Will Tell - An Easter Play
Even Me - A Christmas Play For Your
Sunday School

All I Need Is Love - A Play For Teens
Lost And Found - A Children's Christmas
Play
Gotta Love It - A Humorous Play About
Rural Life
<u>How - To Books</u>
How To Make Eye Catching Ebook Covers
Easily

DEDICATION

...For all those teenagers who are suffering. May you experience the awesome love of Jesus Christ!

Table of Contents

SUMMARY

Time Will Tell is a short drama about a teenage girl named April who lives on the street. Her friend Lisa has invited her to come along to youth group one evening.

The scene opens with Lisa standing at the bus stop waiting for April. There is a terrible storm beginning, with pouring rain and thunder and lightning. April arrives late at the bus stop and inevitably declines Lisa's invitation. Lisa however is not very happy with April and still tries to persuade her to come. In their discussion, Lisa tells April about Jesus Christ and his death, leaving April confused and doubtful.

The storm worsens while thunder and lightning flash…and everything goes dark.

The two girls find themselves back in time to witness the crucifixion of Jesus Christ firsthand.

As the story unfolds, April is thrown into a spiritual struggle to determine the reality of her own sinful nature.

April, through observing the crucifixion herself, and with the help of her friend Lisa, decides to make a decision for Christ.

Props, special effects, costumes needed:

– Sounds of rain, thunder, lightning and clothes (sound effects are tape-recorded)
– Dry ice (optional for fog to show time travel)
– Spotlight and disco light (round ball that looks like stars)
– Easter song (something played as Jesus carries his cross)
– Wooden cross with foot stand and nails
– Two soldier's outfits with two hammers and nails

– Costume for Jesus (torn robe, crown of thorns, sandals etc.)

– Umbrella and rain jacket for Lisa

– Black leather jacket and boots with bandanna for April

– Bus stop sign

– Three large rocks (cut out of cardboard) for scenery

CHARACTERS

Lisa –

She is a teenage girl who is typically dressed. She attends the local youth group. She's a nice girl.

April –

A bad street girl dressed roughly.

Soldiers –

Two or three soldiers. They crucify Christ. They have no speaking parts. (You can actually use as many soldiers as you like)

Jesus Christ –

Plays the part of Jesus Christ being crucified. Must be a mature student or adult.

Angels –

As many as you like. No speaking parts. They just dance.

Sound and light man –
In charge of playing tape recorded music in various parts throughout the play, also works the lights for the stage.

(The part of Lisa and April can be played as two guys instead, or one guy and one girl. It is up to you. All you have to do is change names)

SCENE ONE

Scene opens with bus stop sign at center stage. The rain begins to pour, and thunder and lightning flash just as Lisa gets to the bus stop. (Soundman works special effects here: rain, thunder, flashes of lightning, and Spotlight)

Lisa enters the stage all wet with jacket on and hair wet. She opens her umbrella but it won't work right. Giving up on it, she stands in place with hands in pockets jigging up and down. She appears to be annoyed as she waits patiently in the rain for her friend April to meet her.

Lisa –
Where is she? (Impatiently annoyed)… Man, were going to miss the bus. (Looks at watch)

(Thunder and lightning again)
(April enters and walks like a punk, as if she doesn't care. Her hair is also wet)

Lisa –
April, what took you so long? I started to think you changed your mind.

April –
Well actually, I did, I'm not going.

Lisa –
What…? What do you mean you're not going?

April –
I'm not going! I… I just decided not to.

Lisa –
April…(Very disappointed)…You told me you would go to youth group with me this time.

April –
(Snappy) Well I can't!

Lisa –

Why?

April –

Because…(Sighs)…I'm not like you guys.

Lisa –

What do you mean April?… You are too.

April –

(Sarcastically) Oh yeah, like I'm really like you guys. (Getting mad) I live on the street! Do you know what that's like Lisa? You and your religious friends…You don't understand…You have no idea!

Lisa –

Okay fine…so we don't all live on the street…But I told you before that that doesn't matter.

April –

(Upset) It does matter! It matters to me! I feel like I'm not good enough when I'm with you guys, like I'm supposed to be perfect or something…Well I am far from perfect… MY LIFE SUCKS!

Lisa –

(Sympathetic) April…(She sighs) you think I'm perfect? I'm not perfect either. Just because I'm a Christian doesn't mean I'm better than you. My life isn't that great either. I've done a lot of stupid things…The ONLY (With great emphasis) reason I am who I am today is because of Jesus Christ!

April –

Yeah…and you guys are always talking about Jesus Christ. Like he's supposed to be my father or something…Well I'll tell you about my father. He meant everything to me, I LOVED HIM! (Emotional)…and then he left me.

Lisa –

Well Jesus would never leave you. Once you got him in your heart, you're his forever.

April –

(Annoyed) I don't even know what that means. For all I know you could be making this junk up right now. How could some guy that lived a long time ago mean anything to me now, hugh?

Lisa –

He isn't just some guy, he's God! That's what the Bible says. I didn't make anything up. I know for a fact that Jesus would do ANYTHING for you!

April –

(Sarcastically) Anything? That's a good one. What has this JESUS done for me lately?

Lisa –

He died for you!

April –

He died for me…(A question but meant as a sarcastic statement)… Like I'm supposed to know what that means.

Lisa –
(Sympathetic) Oh April…I wish I could get you to understand somehow.

(Just at that time, flashes of lightning and loud crashes of thunder cause the stage to go dark. The church/auditorium lights must be off too. All is dark except for strobe lights or disco lights that come on above, giving the illusion that something weird is happening: They are going back in time)

END OF SCENE ONE

SCENE TWO

(Bus stop sign is gone. All props from scene one have been removed) Spotlights come back on the stage. The two girls stand up. They are confused and shaken. They straighten themselves up as they look around. (Dry ice may be added here as a special effect. It will give the appearance of time travel)

April –
What happened?

Lisa –
I don't know…(Looks around)

…I don't know!

April –
(Looking around as well) I think I hear something…Shhhh…It sounds like someone's coming.

Lisa –
Come on, we better hide.

(The two girls hide behind a rock on the stage)

(Music begins. A song about the crucifixion or a sad Easter song is played. You can also play music with no words. From the back of the church/auditorium enters Jesus. He is pulling his cross on his back while two soldiers follow behind him. Jesus has a crown of thorns and a tattered robe that is ripped into shreds on his back from being whipped repeatedly. The two girls stay hidden as they watch Jesus drag the cross up to the front. The music stops)

(The soldiers put Jesus up on the cross and nail his hands and feet, then they exit. As the soldiers exit, April stands up)

April –
What's going on?… Who is this?

Lisa –
(Joining her and pointing) This?…THIS IS JESUS CHRIST!

April –
Well, what's he doing on a cross?

Lisa –
Dying…for you!

Jesus Christ –
(Calls to April)… April…April! I have brought you here so that you may understand.

April –
(Steps Out from behind the rock) Understand? I DON'T understand.

Jesus Christ –
April, I am suffering for YOU. I am dying for YOUR sins.

April –
What do you mean? I don't want you to die.

Jesus Christ –
I must die…but I will live again!

April –
(Very upset) NO! NO! I am not going to let you die right here in front of me…(Looks around) Somebody…Lisa…Help me! Help me get him down.

Lisa –
April…He has to do this for you…and for me…for everyone!

April –
Jesus? What do you want me to do then, stand here?

Jesus Christ –

No my child, you must repent of your ways. Give your sins to me and I will take your punishment for you.

April –
But why would you do that? (Starts to cry)

Jesus Christ –
Because I love you!

April –
(Hangs head down and sobs into her hands. Then looks up as she sniffles) I'm sorry Jesus. I never knew. I didn't know that you loved ME. I'm sorry. I'm sorry for all the rotten things I've done. I'm sorry I'm so messed up. I'm sorry I did this to you. (Sobs heavily) I'm sorry. I'm sorry! (As April repents, suitable music is played)

Lisa –
(Joins her friend to comfort her.)
(The music turns into angelic music as many angels dance around April, Lisa, and Jesus, at the foot of the cross. They smile at the Angels

celebrating April's decision for Christ. Then the angels exit. As the song ends, April and Lisa look up at the sky. Thunder and lightning begin again, and with one big bang, all goes dark. They go forward in time to their present day)

END OF SCENE TWO

SCENE THREE

As the scene changes and time goes back to the present day, props are changed. Jesus, the cross, and rocks are removed. Spotlight is turned on again pointing at Lisa and April. They are lying down on the floor of the stage and slowly get Up.

April –
Wow…(Looks around) Lisa, we must be back.

Lisa –
Was that ever AWESOME!…WOW!

(They dust themselves off)

April –
You know Lisa, I never really knew who Jesus was, or what he actually did for me till now.

Lisa –
I'm glad you finally understand.

(Fade appropriate music in here lightly until ending. Then loud as they exit)

April –
Hey Lisa, how about we go to that youth group after all? Let's go catch the bus. What do you say?

Lisa –
I'd say…(pauses for thought)…it's about time!

(They both exit stage)

THE END

ABOUT THE AUTHOR

Award-winning author Kathleen Morris has written numerous articles, poetry, and short stories published in various Saskatchewan newspapers. Her poem *Refuge* is published in a book anthology titled *A Golden Morning*. She has written many plays and skits including her play titled *Gotta Love It*, winner of Dancing Sky Theatre's rural writing contest in 2001 where it was also performed by the theatre troupe in Meacham, Saskatchewan.

Deep Bay Vengeance is Kathleen's first novel followed by its sequel *Deep Bay Relic*. When she's not writing, she enjoys spending time with her husband Barry and their three grown children at her home in Saskatchewan, Canada. For more on Kathleen Morris please check out her Author Page at Amazon.com.

OTHER BOOKS BY KATHLEEN MORRIS

<u>Deep Bay Series</u>
Deep Bay Vengeance
Deep Bay Relic
Deep Bay Legacy (Coming 2014)
<u>Blood War Series</u>
The Prion Attachment
Blood Purge (Coming 2014)
<u>Short Inspirations Series</u>
Size Seven Shorts
Short End Of The Stick
Shortcut To Alaska
<u>Short Stories</u>
Along The Way - 12 Short Stories You Can
Read Along The Way
<u>Plays</u>
Time Will Tell - An Easter Play
Even Me - A Christmas Play For Your
Sunday School
All I Need Is Love - A Play For Teens

Lost And Found - A Children's Christmas Play

Gotta Love It - A Humorous Play About Rural Life

How - To Books

How To Make Eye Catching Ebook Covers Easily

www.ingramcontent.com/pod-product-compliance
Lightning Source LLC
LaVergne TN
LVHW051819080426
835513LV00017B/2016